i

Transactional Analysis for Everybody Series

TA for TOTS VOL. II

by Alvyn M. Freed, Ph.D.

JALMAR PRESS INC.

Printed in the United States of America

Library of Congress Catalog Number 77-375665

ISBN: 0-915190-25-7

Illustrations

by

JoAnn
Dick

v

~DEDICATION~

To TOTS and PRINZES
everywhere who
are discovering
OKness in themselves
      and others,
         leading thus
            to joy and
               contentedness.

ACKNOWLEDGEMENTS

To JALMAR employees one and all who, through their work, loyalty and spontaneity inspire me to greater effort!

(in alphabetical order):

Sue Baker

Marge Freed

Cheri Johnson

Suzanne Mikesell

Pat Pittsley

Marge Thomas

Joan Whiteley

Phyllis Williams

Special thanks also to: Ron Dick, Bob Erdmann & Sharon Schultz

ix

CONTENTS

INTRODUCTION

The wonderful response to TA for TOTS (and other prinzes) has prompted me to write TA for TOTS, VOL.II. In TA for TOTS (and other prinzes) I discussed only a few of the many feelings people have, such as anger, fear and confusion, as well as the more positive affect of love through strokes. A whole new generation of

TOTS has arisen since its first printing in 1973. The effort in the present volume is to deal with other important feelings with which youngsters and grown-ups have difficulty, such as hurt, greed, shyness, frustration, OK-ness and others.

Like its predecessor, TA for TOTS, VOL. II aims to strengthen individual feelings of self-worth and to stimulate small group discussion by TOT-groups

(pre-school through fourth grade). If TOTS
and grown-ups can learn to accept and
handle their own feelings without malice
or anxiety, they will be more effective
in dealing with the other important
people in their lives.

I hope my first generation fans will
enjoy seeing some of their old friends,
such as Rocko and Maurice, as they
mingle here in TA for TOTS, VOL. II with

new characters, as these are per-
ceived and brought to life by the
fertile mind and creative skills of
JoAnn Dick.

Alwyn M Freed

Chapter 1

A REVIEW OF T.A. for TOTS and other Prinzes

For you who are now read-ing **TA** for **TOTS**, **VOL. II** and may not have read **TA** for **TOTS** (and other prinze I will tell you what **TA** for **TOTS** was about. I hope that you who already know **TA** for **TOTS** will enjoy this review, too.

In **TA** for **TOTS** I said that all people are animals.

2

Well, we're not vegetables or minerals...

...and like other animals, we eat, sleep, breathe, have feelings, run, play and do all kinds of things.

But as humans, we have within us three different people:

A PARENT, AN ADULT and A CHILD

PARENT: This part believes and behaves as our mothers, fathers and other important people taught us.

ADULT: This part lets us think learn and make sense.

CHILD: This part of us feels, gets angry, hurt or afraid, has fun and feels happy.

4

The CHILD is the part of us that can imagine, invent and play.

The message of TA for TOTS is "YOU ARE OK". That means you can think and do things. It means you are worthwhile and important to yourself and to other people in your life: mother, father, brothers, sisters, grand-parents, teachers.

YOU ARE OK

You were OK when you were born and have been ever since. Believe in yourself, love yourself, love other people and you will be happy.

In TA for TOTS, I told about WARM FUZZIES and COLD PRICKLIES.

6

WARM FUZZIES are the many things we say and do for each other that help us feel safe and **OK**...

...a friendly smile, a kind word, a helping hand, a hug, a kiss, a back scratch.

WARM FUZZIES keep us healthy and happy.

Unhappy feelings happen when **COLD PRICKLIES** show up.(Brrr...

7

Brrr~ I get goose bumps just thinking about Cold Pricklies.)
   Have you ever been made fun of or yelled at or hit? Ouch! Those were Cold Pricklies.
   In TA for TOTS, I said that we can feel better by asking for WARM FUZZIES, by talking about our feelings, and by knowing that we are OK.

8

It is important to know how
to handle your feelings.
Maybe TA for TOTS
or TA for TOTS, VOL. II
will help you.
I hope so. Let me
know if they do.

9

Meanwhile, I wish you a good life filled with **WARM FUZZIES** and **OK** feelings

I hope you enjoy this book, Maybe someday, you will read **TA** for **TOTS** and enjoy it too.

Your friend,

Al Freed

Chapter 2

FEELING HAPPY

HAPPINESS...

everyone is
entitled
to the pursuit
of happiness!

Now I've <u>got</u> it!

HAPPINESS

Tum s
de s
dum s

...but just can't
seem to hold
onto it.

We forget that Happiness is a _feeling_. It's not a thing we can buy or get as a gift.

15

the going!" it said. I liked that! I liked that!

"The fun is in " the going."

Beep!
Beep

Think about that.
It's often not so much having things as it is <u>doing</u> things that brings happy feelings.

17

Happiness is a feeling that often shows up when we do good, fun things such as: PLAYING CHASE, TUMBLING DOWN A

18

There are all kinds
of things you can do
that are fun...

...Fix
SOMETHING GOOD TO EAT

I think I'll
have a spot
of "T"

DRAW SOME FUZZIES AND SEND THEM TO SOMEONE.

BUILD A SAND CASTLE

MAKE THINGS with scraps

21

DOING GOOD THINGS is a key that can unlock the WARM FUZZIES and let them

22

24

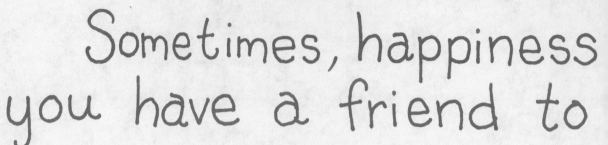

Sometimes, happiness
you have a friend to

26

is just knowing ~~talk~~ to and play with.

Tie big knots on the ends of the string so it can't pull loose! Then... wax the string and pull it very tight.

27

Here's a **HAPPY** thing to do right now: Give someone a WARM

FUZZY

Say something nice to someone near you.

Help someone else feel happy and you'll feel happy too!

29

32

Sometimes HURT FEELINGS happen

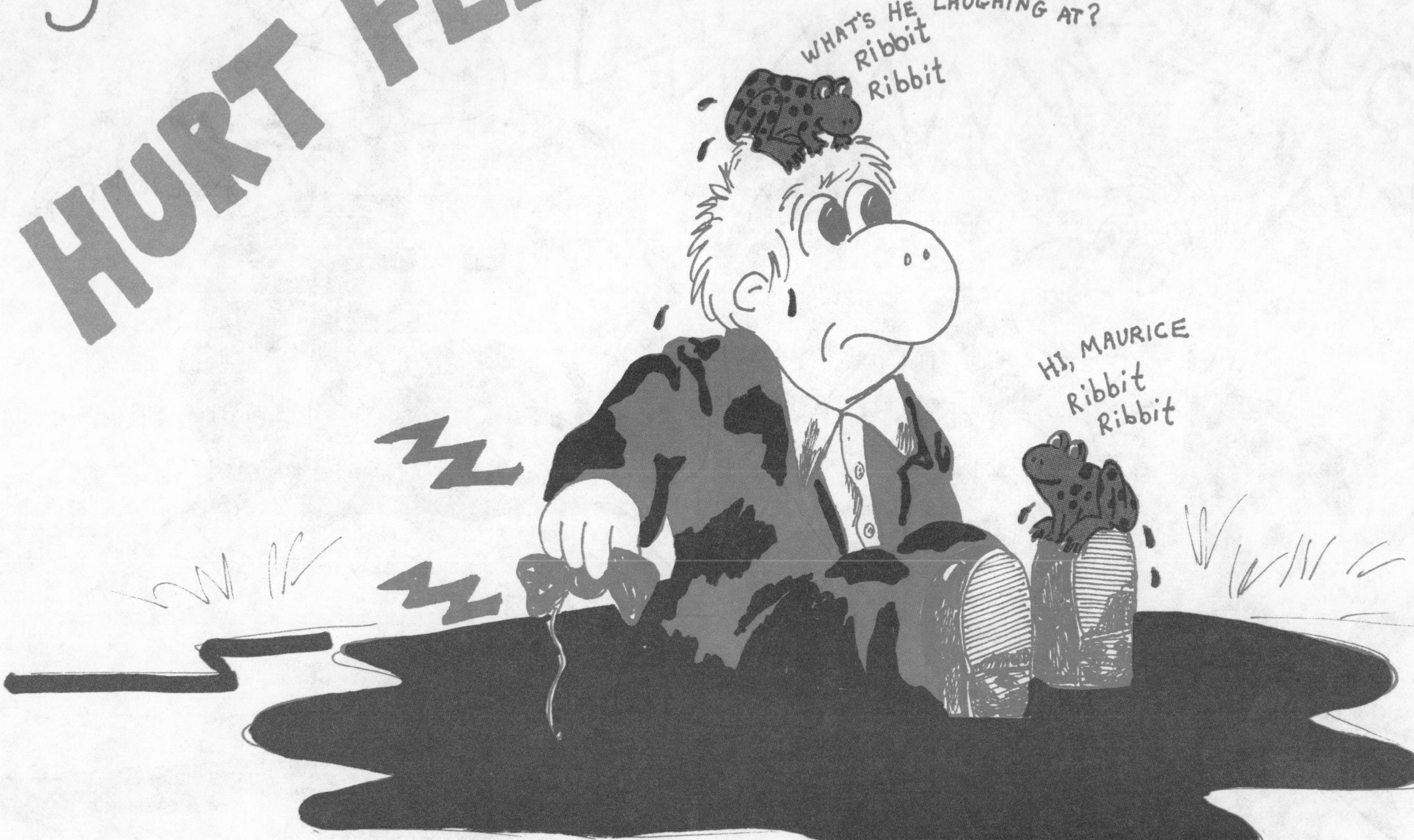

when friends laugh at you...

Ha, ha, ha

You look so funny!

ha, ha, ha

You wore a suit to go frog hunting!

ha, ha, ha...

35

HURT FEELINGS

may happen when Dad and Mom get angry at you...

... over what you did (or didn't do).

37

When you have Hurt Feelings, you feel angry...

... or sad...... or not O.K.

When your feelings are hurt...

...you might get angry and call people names...

...or hide from them and sulk and feel unhappy all by yourself,

but those are sad, COLD PRICKLY things to do.

It is better for you to let people know how you feel.

That is because no one can "read your mind". Even your family or your best friends cannot tell for sure how you feel or what you think unless <u>you</u> tell them.

Abracadabra, alacazam... tell me why Maurice is mad at me.

42

A good thing to do would
be to talk about your hurt
feelings.
Tell the person that you didn't
like what he or she said or did.

Then, tell that person what you wish they would do or say...

I wanted you to say go<u>o</u>d things ... like "nice suit"...

... or "Golly, I hope your shell isn't broken!"

THERE HE GOES, WORRYING ABOUT HIS SHELL AGAIN!

44

...<u>you</u> will feel better if you talk things over, and the people who listen may stop doing some of those things you felt bad about.

Golly, I guess I didn't even think about how you felt! I'm sorry!

That's O.K. Rocko...

It was no fun being mad at my best friend!

46

Chapter 4

QUIT
or
WIN
you have a choice

king was ready to give up and surrender his army and country to the enemy.

he saw a spider trying
to spin a web.

53

On the first try the spider went too high

54

On the fifth try it
did it's best but
went too far west...

...and on the sixth,
the little beast
went too far east!

57

Then, on the <u>seventh</u>
try, the spider caught the

58

twig and was able to spin its' web.

The king decided that if a little spider could try over and over until it succeeded...

...then he, a great king,
could try again too.

He got his troops together
and tried again to win
the battle.

He did win, and the history of his country was changed from what it might have been if he had given up.

63

Did you ever feel like that king? Have you ever wanted to just give up...

...perhaps when you first tried to get dressed all by yourself or when you were learning to tie your shoes?

65

Did you ever feel like giving up when something was very hard for you to do?

pouring a glass of milk... doing math...

...or spelling or learning to play music?

skreee
skreee

68

and someone told you:
JUST PRACTICE!
you'll get it !

You may need to change something you do wrong...
... or learn something that is new to you.

If you can't tell what you are doing wrong and you practice the wrong way,

then that can make the "wrong way" hard to change.

When something is <u>too</u> hard to do,

DON'T GIVE UP!

Keep on trying, but get
some help from Mom, Dad, your
teacher or a friend who is
good at doing the thing you
want to learn.

72

Have that person check to see if you are making any mistakes.

73

Practice the <u>right</u> way over and over and you will get better and better at doing what you are learning.

75

Chapter 5

Hmmm,
THIS LOOKS LIKE
THE WORK OF
GEORGE FUZZINGTON.

HONESTY

"Where did you get it?" asked Mother.

"On the front steps of Johnny's house", I said.

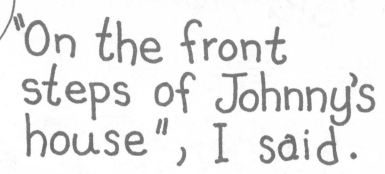

I did not like it at all when she told me it was probably Johnny's and I should take it back.

79

"But I found it!"
I told her.

"You found it where it wasn't lost," she said, "so take it back and put it on Johnnys' porch.

That is the honest thing to do."

"But somebody else might take it!" I said.

Mother told me "That isn't your worry; your worry is to be honest and not to take something that doesn't belong to you."

"If it isn't yours,
  don't take it.
        It's only yours when
        it's given to you or
        when you buy it."

I felt unhappy,
  but I took the gun
        back where I
        had found it.

That's nice.

People like you when you are honest.

Being honest means leaving other people's things alone...

or your friend's money...

...even your sister's yummy chocolate chip cookie...

...or your brother's new toy

Being honest also means telling

When people find out

that you haven't told them the truth, they are angry and you are unhappy and ashamed.

chomp!

Those are COLD PRICKLY feelings, much worse than telling the truth in the first place.

When you are honest,
people will trust you
and like you....

Love is feeling safe

Chapter 6

When Maurice was very young, there was a time when he did not like himself much at all. The COLD PRICKLY feeling began

Yech! I hate being me. I wish I was a Giraffe!

A WHAT?

WAAAAA
WAAAA
Now look what you made me do! Mommy's nice cup is all broken!

Mom felt very sad.
Then she got mad
and Maurice was scared.

WAAAA
WAAA

Maurice felt sad
because the
pretty cup was
broken
        and he felt angry at himself
                    because he had not
                            told the truth.

He did not like himself(and he was afraid that no one else liked him either).

DO YOU REALLY LOVE ME?

DO YOU LOVE ME?

Maurice asked his Mommy and Daddy over and over.

102

He wanted people to tell
him he was loved,
   no matter what he
   thought or did.

Of course, they always said "Yes, we love you" (because they did love him dearly).

Gee! I'm not so bad. They do still love me!

That helped him feel OK about himself.

But then, just as he began
to feel WARM and FUZZY
and SAFE

Maurice would think of
COLD PRICKLY things...

BRRRR

Have you ever felt that way?

"Brrrr"

I have!   "Brrrr"

Sometimes, people just get to feeling very unhappy with themselves, `ouch`! even when they have not done anything wrong.

108

ugg!

ssssst

sssst

Well, you can't really spray
cold pricklies away like that,
but there is a good
way you can get rid of
COLD PRICKLIES
and feel OK again!

CHASE
COLD PRICKLIES
X
AWAY
SPRAY
NON-AEROSOL

WIN
BRAND

109

Remember, a way to feel better is to talk about what happened and tell how you are feeling.

Talk to people you like and trust.

Dad, I sure wish I could be a giraffe!

A giraffe Maurice?

Talk to people who like you and who will take time to listen to what you say.

That is just what
Maurice did.

He told his Mother
how he broke the
tea cup and how
he felt worried.

The person you talk to may
not act happy about what
you tell them,

   but they will still love you,

and you will feel better.

114

Son,
I was angry
when my
old tea cup
got broken...

..but I'm very
happy that
you told me
the truth!

Maurice began to like himself
again. He felt safe and happy.

He knew that he
He felt safe
and safe

I'll never forget about the time when I was two years old.

I was happy as I could be, dressed in a nice warm cocoon of a suit, with mittens on my little hands...

Look! He's as happy as a clam at high tide!

120

Mother took my cousin Leonard and me to my favorite place, the corner bakery.

I liked the bakery because Mrs. Grady, the nice bakery lady, always gave me a "lady finger," which I loved.

A lady finger is a yummy little cake.

That day was special,
she gave me
<u>two</u> of the
little cakes.

Thank you!

I was so
happy!

124

What I didn't know was that because my cousin Leonard was there, I was supposed to turn around and give one of the lady fingers to him...

...but I didn't know that. In fact...

Yum! Yum!

I didn't like the idea at all when Mother suggested it.

I clung even tighter to the two cakes and marched proudly out of the store.

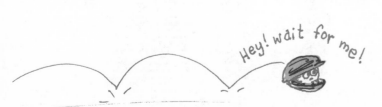

Hey! wait for me!

127

Mother took <u>both</u> cakes, gave one to Len, and <u>threw</u> the other one into the street.

It landed right in a puddle of mud!

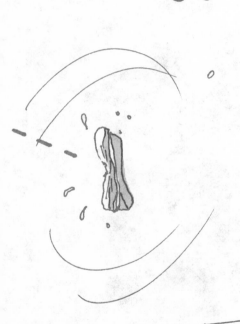

I can't look.

My joy was dashed!
Helplessness and sorrow
filled my eyes with tears.

130

My lady finger was gone forever, thrown into the  dirty street.

Mom said she taught me something that day. She said I learned to be more generous.

131

I'm not sure. I didn't <u>feel</u> more generous. I learned to share, I guess, but I wonder if that was the best way to teach it.

Help!

I know I'll never forget the sight of that beautiful lady finger flying out into the street.

Little boy's broken heart

133

How did <u>you</u> learn to share, or to be generous?

Or are you still <u>greedy</u>?

What do you think about <u>sharing</u>?

How do you feel when people share things with you?

Try it and see.

135

Chapter 8
PETS

Pets are fun.

We love them...

They snuggle right
up and warm us,
no matter how
other people
may be
treating us.

In fact, some of them
seem to know when
we feel unhappy or
ill and then they
love us most.

142

Do you think pets know when we are sad and need a WARM FUZZY?

I think some of them do. Do you think so?

143

The dogs I've had showed parent, adult and child

parts of their thinking

Duke I and Duke II showed me their fun (child) side when they ran after a stick.

Duke II kept our 18 month old son Larry from wandering too close to the ocean.

Do any of your pets
show a parent, adult
and child?
Tell how.

What do they do
that lets you know
they love you, are
smart, have fun and
protect you?

How do you show your pets that you love and care for them? Do you feed them and keep them clean—even at times when you might not wish to?

149

Most pets can't protect you.
They need <u>you</u> to protect
them and take care of them.
150

By loving and caring for pets, you learn to be a gentle and loving person.

Your animals will learn to like and trust you and you will like yourself and other people.

151

Chapter 9

Do you ever feel **Shy**?
Most people do feel
shy once in a
while.

When grown-
ups see a child
acting shy they
often say something like,
"My, oh my, you are so shy".

Hello, Roopie! Welcome to Fida's birthday party. Oh, look. He's shy. Isn't he cute.

154

Yes, my little Roopie is so shy...

Sometimes, when we hear people **say** we are shy, we feel even **more shy!**

Why do you think that happens?

155

I think it happens because when we are very young, we believe that everything people say about us is

I didn't know I was shy!

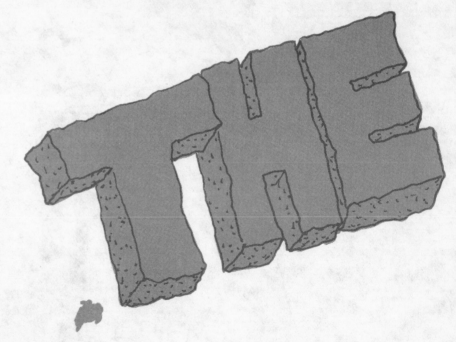

So, when we hear grown-ups say that we are shy, we think we must <u>be</u> shy (even if we're not sure what that word "shy" means).

157

Some grown-ups like children to behave in a shy way. They think that it will keep them from being too noisy, pushy or greedy.

They hope that shyness will stop children from doing things that could be harmful or dangerous.

But, we don't need to feel shy to be polite and kind to other people.

Yes, please.

Thank you.

It's your turn.

We don't need to feel shy in order to be careful and safe from danger.

Hey! You! Want a ride?

Don't talk to strangers.

DADDY, MOMMY!

she's not SHY, she's careful.

161

Don't be so **SHY** Roopie! Go have fun at Fida's party.

Oddly, those us to <u>stop</u>

SHYNESS is an unhappy, painful feeling. A person who feels shy much of the time may be

very same people who teach
act shy often wish we would
acting so shy!

afraid to make friends and have fun.

People who feel shy may be afraid to ask for things they need or want.

SHY is being afraid that other people won't like you – even before they get to know you.

It's sort of like not taking a nice gift because you're afraid you might lose it.

165

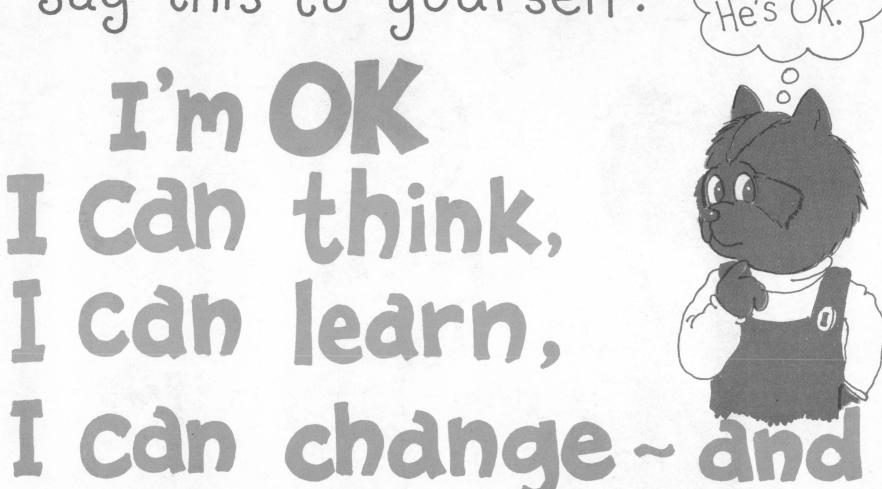

Think about what you will say or do. Then **BE BRAVE** and do it!

What can I say?

Try it and see what happens.

other people are OK too!

168

Give yourself some
nice big, shaggy

WARM FUZZIES

just for being brave
enough to do whatever
it was you felt shy about.

169

Sometimes, things might not go as you hope they will. You may make mistakes.

170

Don't worry about that.
Forget your mistakes.
Think about how you will do better
next time. Keep track of the times
you do right. You will find that
as you **DO** things and get to know
more people, you will feel less and less
SHY and more and more **OK**.

have lots of fun.

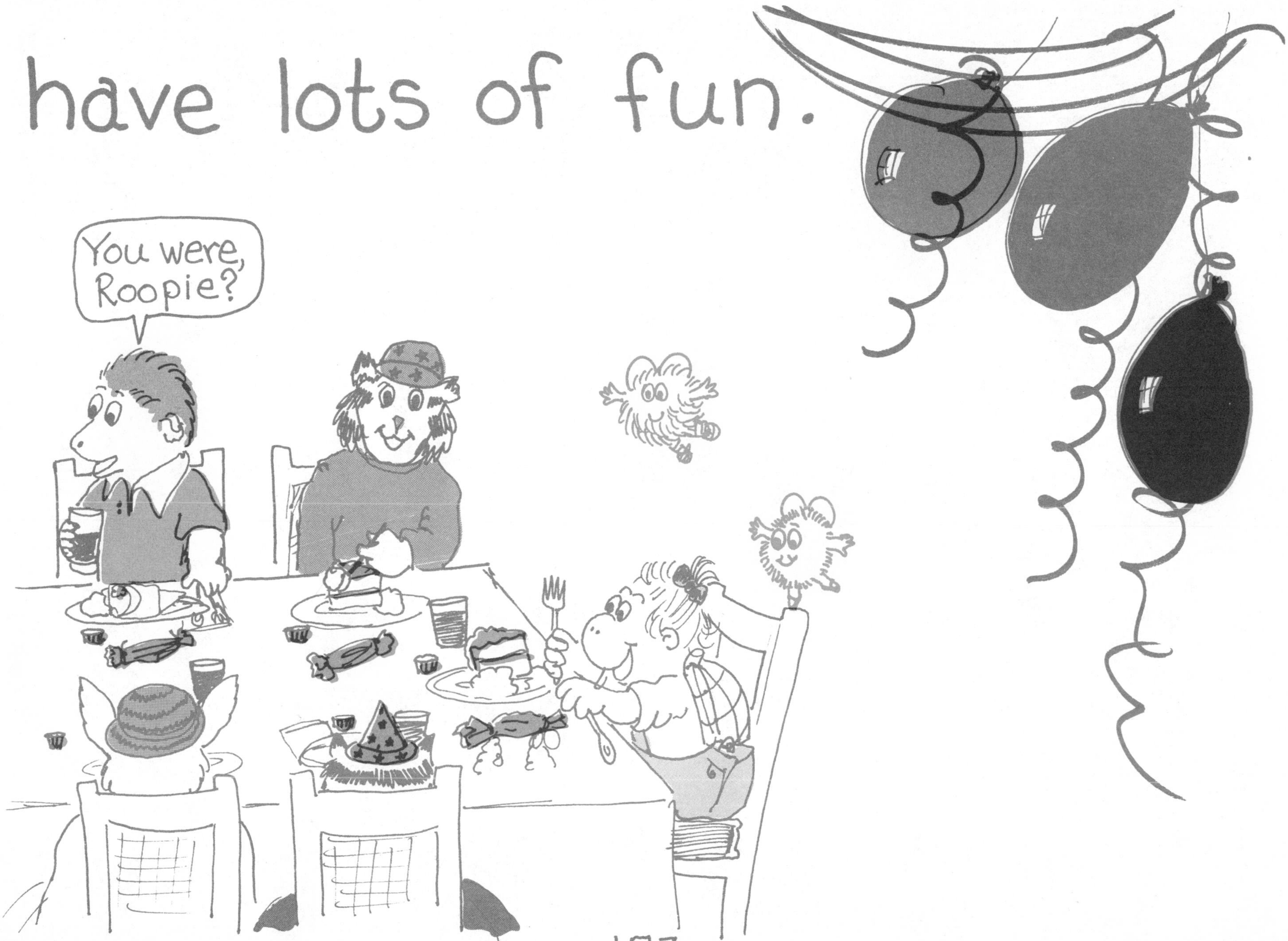

Chapter 10

I'M OK

Are you?

YES!

176

You

are

OK

You always
have been
OK

177

You Are Good

You can think
and learn
and change.
YOU are
worthwhile
to yourself and

178

think things
not good enough.
Everyone can do better than I
can. I'm not smart.
It's no use to even try ".

181

Have you ever felt that way?
I have. Sometimes I **YELL** at

grrrl

Slam!

people or
slam doors
or sulk...

yipe!

...but I know I'm still **OK**
and I work hard
at being a good person.
I think that is
important.

Being OK doesn't mean you'll never feel angry or sad or hurt. It doesn't mean everything people do is right or helpful. Sometimes people do things that are harmful to other people and themselves. Sometimes you must be careful who you trust.

ouch!

Being OK <u>does</u> mean that you can think and learn from your mistakes. You can change and do better next time.

So keep telling

I AM GOOD -

You
to

yourself

I AM OK!

will begin
feel good about
yourself and other
people too.

You
are OK!

In **TA** for **TOTS** there are some "magic words" People liked them so well that we made a poster out of them.

Today I'm O.K.

Say these "magic words" each morning and night while you look in your magic mirror in the bathroom and you will be an OKayan.

Today I'm Okay.
so are they.
Today I'm a Prinz.
So are they.

Today I will give
ten Warm Fuzzies away.

Today is now.
Today I'm OK.

THE Warm Fuzzy CLUB

BE A MEMBER!

JOIN OUR CLUB!

All those in favor of feeling OK and feeling loved are WARM FUZZY people. The WARM FUZZY CLUB is dedicated to keeping WARM FUZZIES alive and bouncing. You can get more WARM FUZZIES and be a WARM FUZZY person to friends and grown-ups by being a WARM FUZZY CLUB MEMBER.

When you sign up for the WARM FUZZY CLUB you get your WARM FUZZY CLUB Membership Certificate and a WARM FUZZY to wear proudly.

Then, every eight weeks there's the WARM FUZZY CLUB NEWS. The NEWS is written by Dr. and Mrs. Alvyn M. Freed, psychologist, lecturer and author of TA for TOTS, TA for KIDS, and TA for TEENS. Dr. Freed will tell you how to be happier and how to make other people happier with winning WARM FUZZY ways. You'll find out about special WARM FUZZY games and contests, too. Your parents and friends will want to share the WARM FUZZY NEWS because it always contains sprightly, helpful suggestions from Dr. Freed and Marge Freed.

WARM FUZZY CLUB members will receive a free WARM FUZZY, I'm OK full color poster (18" x 24")*. This colorful poster has the wonderful Today, I'm OK poem reprinted from TA for TOTS. The beautiful poster is ringed by all the funny, lovable characters from Dr. Freed's books.

As WARM FUZZY CLUB members you'll be the first to know about new books in the WARM FUZZY series by JALMAR PRESS and you'll be able, if you wish, to take advantage of special offerings before the books or WARM FUZZY mementoes are distributed to the public.

There will be other offerings to club members such as WARM FUZZY ID buttons, WARM FUZZY T-Shirts and more exciting posters. So, if you want to keep WARM FUZZIES alive and bouncing, and forever banish COLD PRICKLIES from OK Land the WARM FUZZY CLUB IS FOR YOU.

SIGN HERE FOR YOUR WARM FUZZY CLUB MEMBERSHIP

Please enroll me as a member of the WARM FUZZY CLUB.
Enclosed is my annual dues for the Club ($4.00)

NAME: _____

STREET _____

CITY: _____ STATE: _____ ZIP: _____

MAIL TO:
WARM FUZZY CLUB
JALMAR Press, Inc.,
6501 Elvas Ave.,
Sacramento, Ca. 95819

JALMAR PRESS, INC.
6501 Elvas Avenue
Sacramento, CA 95819
(916) 451-2897

MINIMUM ORDER: $10.00

Shipping, Handling & Insurance Charges:

Under $15.00	$1.75
$15.00 to $20.00	$2.25
Over $20.00	$2.75
TOT PAC or KID PAC	$4.00

Bill To _____

Street _____

City _____ State _____ Zip _____

PO # _____ Date _____

☐ Master Charge ☐ BankAmericard/Visa

Account # _____

Expiration Date _____

Signature _____

Ship To _____

Street _____

City _____ State _____ Zip _____

ORDER FORM

Order	NEW BOOKS	Retail
	Please Keep on Smoking! (Sept.) PB 0-915190-27-3	$2.95
	Cooking on a Woodburning Stove (Sept) PB 0-915190-28-1	$7.95
	Stress: In The Eye of the Beholder (Oct.) PB 0-915190-29-X	$5.95
	How To Enlarge Your Breasts, Naturally (Oct) PB 0-915190-30-3	$6.95
	BACKLIST	
	Finding Hidden Treasure PB 0-915190-16-8	$6.95
	First Time Out PB 0-915190-26-5	$5.95
	Hope for the Frogs PB 0-915190-17-6	$3.95
	The Human Almanac PB 0-915190-23-0	$9.95
	Joy of Backpacking PB 0-915190-06-0	$5.95
	The Original Warm Fuzzy Tale PB 0-915190-08-7	$3.95
	Pajamas Don't Matter** PB 0-915190-21-4	$5.95
	The Parent Book PB 0-915190-15-X	$9.95
	Reach for the Sky PB 0-915190-13-3	$7.95
	SPIRIT MASTERS for TA for Tots Coloring Book PB 0-915190-18-4	$3.95
	*TA for Kids (3rd Edition) PB 0-915190-09-5	$4.95
	TA for Management PB 0-915190-05-2	$6.95

Order	BACKLIST	Retail
	TA for Teens PB 0-915190-03-6	$7.95
	TA for Tots (And Other Prinzes) PB 0-915190-12-5	$7.95
	HC 0-915190-11-7	$11.95
	Spanish Ed 0-915190-12-5	$7.50
	*TA for Tots, Vol II PB 0-915190-25-7	$8.95
	TA for Tots Coloring Book PB 0-8431-0229-2	$1.95
	A Time to Teach, A Time to Dance HC 0-915190-04-4	$8.95
	The Warm Fuzzy Song Book PB 0-915190-14-1	$3.95
	When Apples Ain't Enough PB 0-915190-24-9	$4.95
	SPECIAL TA BOOKLETS	
	Becoming The Way We Are	$2.95
	Introduce Yourself to TA	$1.25
	Introduce Your Marriage to TA	$1.50
	TA Made Simple	$1.00
	Warm Fuzzy Club Membership	$4.00
	A-V MULTIMEDIA PACS	
	FUN PAC	$14.95
	*KID PAC	$165.00
	PARENT PAC ☐ Cassette ☐ Record	$29.95

A-V MULTIMEDIA PACS	Retail	Order
*TOT PAC ☐ Filmstrips ☐ Slides		$135.00
Warm Fuzzy T-Shirts Children's Sizes: S,M,L,XL		$4.95
Adult Sizes: S,M,L,XL		$5.95
CASSETTES, RECORDS, POSTERS		
The Parent Book 45-minute cassette**		$9.95
TA for Tots 55-minute cassette**		$9.95
TA for Kids 45-minute cassette**		$9.95
TA for Teens 45-minute cassette**		$9.95
TA for Management 45-minute cassette**		$9.95
Songs of the Warm Fuzzy LP Album ("ALL ABOUT YOUR FEELINGS")		$5.95
RELAX FOR HEALTH CASSETTES: Side A: Introduction to Hypnosis / Side B: Induction, Weight Control		$9.95
Side A: Introduction to Hypnosis / Side B: Induction, Tobacco Control		$9.95
Side A: Introduction to Hypnosis / Side B: Induction, Ego Strengthening		$9.95
Today I'm OK (4-color Poster) 6/$5.00		$1.00
Warm Fuzzies (min. order 50)		50 ea.
SUBTOTAL		
MINIMUM ORDER $10.00		
CA Residents add Sales Tax		
Add Shipping Handling		
TOTAL		

*SPECIAL OFFER TO SCHOOLS:
Class Set (min. 20) of TA FOR TOTS, or TA FOR KIDS available at 20% Discount with purchase of KID PAC or TOT PAC.

*Only available from JP in the United States of America

(5096)